CREATION

I0472797

By Lord Loveday Ememe and available from Lulu.
The constitution and policing
Heresy
Starfleet
The supernatural

www.lulu.com

ISBN: 978-1-4710-8936-7

Table of Contents

1. LIFE CAN ONLY BE CREATED BY THE SUPERNATURAL

According to the guidance of the constitution of this planet, earth, which is the Christian principles, civil rights, life, can only be created supernaturally by the uncivilized. The supernatural or the uncivilized might give the impression that the civilized have contributed to the creation of life by the use of their supernatural powers and senses, interpreting physical contact as a contribution, appearances can be deceptive, the whole process regardless of appearance is completely supernatural. This is not to suggest that the uncivilized collectively are females regardless of appearances. But the uncivilized by their own actions are suggesting that they are as a collective females regardless of appearances. This is because they imply that females are the weaker sex, whose responsibilities are to create life and look after children. And the constitution implies that strength is to be associated with the characteristics or qualities of the natural or the civilized. This is quite important in understanding the purpose of a peace keeping force, which according to the guidance of the constitution, confirms that a police force and police training colleges are meant to aspire to the qualities or characteristics of the civilized. Contrary to the misconception of linking the military and police forces to representations of the supernatural, they are according to the guidance of the constitution representations of the civilized.

According to the guidance of the constitution, because life can only be created supernaturally, it can be done in a lot of different ways. According to the guidance of the constitution, the Christian teachings, civil rights, Adam was created supernaturally from sand. Eve could only create life supernaturally because of her uncivilized nature. This will suggest that life can be created supernaturally in a lot of different ways.

Another example is the current supernatural alterations of images on the television screen; although they are meant to be representations of the images of other people, they have characteristics of independent life forms. This according to the constitution means they are independent living beings.

The distinction regarding the creation of life is very important, necessary, because the uncivilized live their lives delusively , at the expense of the mental and physically wellbeing of the civilized, at the expense of international peace and security(law and order), at the expense of their destruction. The main reason for their delusional way of life is because their uncivilized natures make it impossible for them to socialize. They then resort to forcing themselves into social situations when their uncivilized natures are incompatible, which results in hostilities, that threatens international peace and security and is unhealthy for the civilized.

These inconsistencies with the compatibility of their uncivilized natures and life, accounts for their deliberate destruction of the planet, and their terrorism.

Their delusional way of life accounts for the unnecessary inclusion of the civilized in the creation of life, which the constitution confirms can only be done supernaturally by the uncivilized. My experiences confirm that the inclusion is not done for good reasons but with the intention of undermining the constitutional rights of the civilized, in order to create and maintain lawlessness.

The civilized child is naturally a commissioner of police from birth, because of the constitutional requirement to align the living conditions to the constitutional living conditions in the Garden of Eden, in order not to compromise the development and education of the civilized child. When an uncivilized child and a civilized child are created, and the living conditions are altered by the uncivilized pretending to be civilized when they are not, the uncivilized child will be aware of the deception, and the civilized child will not be aware of the deception and the education and development of the civilized child will be seriously compromised. Education for the civilized is not the route to being confirmed as commissioners of police. Education for the civilized is a constitutional entitlement as commissioners of police.

The constitution acknowledges the possibility of the uncivilized initiating direct and indirect contact with the civilized and insists on contacts with the civilized must be always done officially, an official acknowledgement of the civilized as commissioners of police. The constitution does not accept or acknowledge personal relationships with the civilized and the uncivilized, these relationships must be governed by the guidelines of the constitution and the civilized in our role as commissioners of police. This helps regulate the supernatural instincts of the uncivilized, which has the potential to be extremely unhealthy for the civilized and a threat to international peace and security.

The constitutional living conditions of the civilized, guarantees, establishes and maintains a constitutional peace keeping force. According to the guidance of the constitution, the civilized are gods (people without supernatural powers and senses); the uncivilized have misinterpreted the guidance of the constitution because they believe that their supernatural powers and senses make them gods. As a consequence of their wrong interpretation of the constitution, they illegally created unconstitutional laws, the Ten Commandments, for the civilized to obey contrary to the guidance of the constitution. The correct interpretation of the constitution has already established that the civilized are incapable of doing anything wrong (not able to sin), because of the lack of supernatural powers and senses. I believe that it was because of their wrong interpretation of the constitution, coupled with the delusional way they live their lives, that they think they can set up or compromise the civilized by sabotaging our interests in things like films, music by supernaturally altering them. They felt that if the civilized are sinning anyway that they will get away with catering to their sadism by tampering with our interests. They failed to consider the possibility that the civilized are incapable of doing anything wrong. They failed to consider that the constitution will identify them as the source of the problem. They also failed to consider that if the civilized, gods, have taken an interest in things like films and music; it becomes constitutionally impossible to supernaturally alter them without the expressed consent of the civilized. The alterations are according to the guidance of the constitution a serious health hazard for the civilized, which means that the civilized cannot consent to these types of changes to films and music. They will also have an impossible task of claiming that their intentions were for the benefit of the civilized, given their past and continuous illegal persecution of the civilized.

According to the guidance of the constitution, the uncivilized are required to make sure that anything created by them, life or anything else, is not a threat to the civilized or a threat to international peace and security.

According to the guidance of the constitution, creation, including the creation of life can only be done supernaturally. The creation of the world was done supernaturally, this means that creation which is work should only be done by the uncivilized. According to the guidance of the constitution anything created is done or should be done to last. Trees do not need repair; they last for or were created to last indefinitely.

According to the guidance of the constitution, the creation of Eve for Adam, will suggest that sexual intercourse was envisaged as part of their companionship, given the differences in gender. This will also suggest that sexual intercourse was not originally meant to be linked to the creation of life. The civilized nature of Adam will suggest that sexual intercourse is a civil right. It needs to be noted that Eve was created before they were forced out of the Garden of Eden.

This suggests that the subsequent linking of sexual intercourse with the creation of life by the uncivilized is meant to try to undermine the civil rights of the civilized. This means that sex is being used as a weapon by the uncivilized to try to compromise the constitutional authority of the civilized. Working or creation which is meant to be done by the uncivilized has been misinterpreted by the uncivilized to include the civilized contrary to the guidance of the constitution.

The civilized are naturally commissioners of police or monarchs with the civil right of dominion over this planet. It is honorary or symbolic as a representation of the confirmation that the civilized are law enforcement officers or peace makers. This is not work or creation. The role of the civilized is not suggested in anyway by the constitution to mean that the civilized are disabled, if at all, it is the uncivilized that are suggested by the constitution to be disabled hence the need to regulate their activities given their supernatural powers and senses, and the possible threat it poses to the mental and physical wellbeing of the civilized and the possible threat it poses to a civilized society. The conventional practice of uncivilized men trying to woo uncivilized women is to try to aspire to the characteristics or qualities of a civilized man. According to the guidance of the constitution, the uncivilized woman or women will have to prove themselves worthy of companionship with a civilized man. A civilized man does not have to undergo the process of approval the uncivilized man is put through in order to aspire to the qualities or characteristics of a civilized man, because we the civilized are naturally civil.

In any civilized society, the necessary infrastructure which is created supernaturally has to be in place for the civilized to assume command effective immediately to establish and to maintain law and order.

2. CREATION AND THE CREATED ARE GOVERNED BY NATURAL LAW OR THE CIVILIZED.

According to the guidance of the constitution, creation involves the use of supernatural powers and senses; this process needs to be regulated by law because of the possible dangers to the civilized and possible dangers in a civilized society associated with the misuse of supernatural powers and senses.

The constitution anticipated that the needs in a civilized society should have been anticipated by the supernatural and created as a one off, to limit the unnecessary use of supernatural powers and senses. The things created should be made to last, and the things created should not be harmful to the civilized or breach the peace in a civilized society.

The current practice which is unconstitutional involves the uncivilized deliberately creating substandard things so that they at some point will need to be repaired or replaced. This problem gives the uncivilized things to do at the expense of the physical and mental wellbeing of the civilized and at the expense of peace and security. The complete chaos or lawlessness that has engulfed the world at present by the misuse supernatural powers and senses by the uncivilized to harm those they consider weaker than they are is confirmation of the need to restore order by the correct identification, interpretation and application of the constitution of this planet, which is the Christian principles, civil rights.

Natural law is based on the civilized nature of man (the civilized). The legal systems of all the countries in the world are based on the civilized nature of man (the civilized). This legal system is the Christian principles, civil rights. It is not being interpreted correctly by the countries using the system, they might not even be aware that the legal system is the Christian principles, so its application is misguided. According to the guidance of the constitution, the civilized have the civil right of dominion, or civil powers or administrative powers over this planet. This civil right makes the civilized real military experts, the civilized have the natural ability to provide peace and security.

According to the guidance of the constitution, the civilized are naturally capable of controlling the uncivilized to establish and maintain law and order. Law and order comes as a package with the civilized natures of the civilized. If the uncivilized try directly or indirectly to undermine the constitutional authority of the civilized and the civilized are forced out of their sacred position or positions with regard to administrative matters, the civilized will take law and other with them. This is the reasoning behind the creation of hell. The collective systematic persecution of the civilized by the uncivilized will suggest that the civilized and the uncivilized are completely different species. My personal experiences with the uncivilized given my civilized nature and the experiences of slaughtered animals for consumption by the uncivilized will suggest that the civilized are seen by the uncivilized as completely different from them, hence the discrimination and persecution of the civilized by the uncivilized. Much importance is not given to science because creation is done supernaturally by supernatural powers, which highlights the differences even more, no visible link. This distinction applies regardless of race, gender, age, family ties, given the collective persecution of the civilized by the uncivilized.

Science could be an aid to law and order. It will help limit the need for the use of supernatural powers and senses under the guise of helping anyone. The right balance has to be found in order to protect individuality, personal freedom.

Scientific creations or supernatural creations under the order of science should be aligned to the standards established in the Garden of Eden. Things should be made or created to last. Science or creation should not be used as a weapon by the uncivilized to give themselves things to do at the expense of compromising the standards set by the constitution. If you need new things, it should not be because of the bad quality of the old things.

The constitution, which is the Christian principles, civil rights, does not recognize or acknowledge, apologizes from the uncivilized for the misuse of their supernatural powers and senses to harm mentally or physically the civilized. This includes the misuse of their supernatural powers and senses to undermine the constitutional authority of the civilized. The constitution expects the offenders, the uncivilized, responsible for the misuse of their supernatural powers and senses to harm the civilized mentally or physically to be severely punished.

The uncivilized by their discriminatory practices towards the civilized, which is extremely severe, and their obvious disregard for the welfare of species different from them, animals, confirm that the civilized are of a different species from them the uncivilized, this means under no circumstances are they to assume the constitutional duties or responsibilities of the civilized.

According to the guidance of the constitution, the civilized in our role as commissioners of police, represent the welfare of all species, which is being deliberately misrepresented by the uncivilized pretending to be civilized, with the intention of assuming the role of commissioners of police meant for the civilized.

Science can be used to provide goods and services in an orderly manner with no effort with technologies like replicators. Replicators are a more advanced way of providing processed food through technology.

Given the extremely hostile behaviour of the uncivilized towards species that are different from them, they should not be allowed to have pets. The practice of the uncivilized to keep animals as pet is presumptuous of them, to think that the animals kept as pets will prefer their company rather than the company of their own species. Any contact the uncivilized initiate with the civilized outside protocols outlined by the constitution is forced or political, show with no substance, aim at giving a false impression, in order to continue their unlawful persecution and domination of those different from them. The purpose of the law is to regulate the supernatural actions or instincts of the uncivilized because of the possible dangers of their supernatural powers and senses to the vulnerable and to a civilized society.

The presumptuous attitude of the uncivilized, conceived by the delusional way they live their lives, made them create the misconception that the civilized want to have anything to do with them. They force this misconception by giving a false impression collectively that there must be something wrong with the civilized if the civilized try to avoid having contact with them. They expect the civilized to like them even when the civilized are being persecuted by the uncivilized. This is a completely impossible expectation that can only be conceived by the uncivilized because of the delusional way they live their lives.

The supernatural instinct of the uncivilized guides them when they create things supernaturally. And because of the possible dangers to the civilized and the possible dangers to a civilized society when exposed to the supernatural instincts of the uncivilized, that is the reason for a constitution to regulate the use of supernatural powers and senses.

According to the guidance of the constitution, the guidelines outlined by the constitution regarding contact with the civilized by the uncivilized is very strict, any deviation from the guidelines by the uncivilized will be severely punished. This is because of the extremely hostile nature of the uncivilized which is always a constant threat to the civilized and always a constant threat to international peace and security. The added problem the uncivilized have with their nature is that it limits their ability to comprehend the horrific effects of the misuse of their supernatural powers and senses on the civilized. They are aware that they are not allowed to misuse their supernatural powers and senses to harm the civilized, but they have ignored the guidance of the constitution because of the delusional way they live their lives. They think that because they pretend to be of the civilized nature when they are not, they can judge correctly the effects of the misuse of their supernatural powers and senses on the civilized. The excesses of their uncivilized nature or constitution will make it impossible for them to judge correctly the real effects of their abusive actions on the civilized. That is the reason for the constitution, to help guide them.

Contrary to the guidance or instruction of the constitution, the world and its inhabitants that are different from the uncivilized are being held hostage or are slaves to the barbarism of the uncivilized, which is creating hell on earth.

Contrary to the guidance of the constitution the uncivilized keep animals as pets because they believe that they are superior to the animals. This superiority complex of the uncivilized accounts for their abusive behaviour towards those that are different from them. According to the guidance of the constitution, the civilized have the right of way or the right of stay over the uncivilized in the world. African Americans use the word tripping in reference to someone being intoxicated by their delusion of self- importance. This is relevant with the attitude of the uncivilized towards the civilized. The uncivilized misuse their supernatural powers and senses to force contact with the civilized outside the stipulated guidelines of the constitution, in order to power trip at the expense of the mental and physical wellbeing of the civilized. If the civilized do the right thing and try to avoid contact with them, the uncivilized see the situation as a challenge that they must win. And given the differences in their uncivilized nature and the civilized nature of the civilized, this will only be interpreted by the constitution as an unlawful attack on the civilized by the uncivilized. There is nothing inviting or attractive about the uncivilized for the civilized, which has been confirmed by the constitution.

The provocative behaviour of the uncivilized includes trying to give the impression that abusive situations created by them, is a favour or a delusional act of kindness. They also give the impression that because they are capable of doing serious damage to the civilized, the civilized should be grateful for minor abuses from them. The constitution does not allow or permit any type of abuse minor or not involving the misuse of supernatural powers and senses by the uncivilized to harm the civilized mentally or physically. The rejection of the uncivilized by the civilized and the constitution is justified.

The uncivilized want to present themselves in a way the civilized and the constitution do not acknowledge. To achieve this they contradict their objectives by using force to force the civilized to have unwanted, unnecessary and unhealthy contact with the uncivilized for unlawful political reasons, in order to continue to unlawfully deny the civilized our constitutional roles as commissioners of police.

Sports is as close to being friendly as the uncivilized can be, but the principle of sports is to defeat your opponent, it is based on conflict. There are safety measures they developed for each sport to make it safe. But the uncivilized nature of the uncivilized is not even suited for games, because their uncivilized nature is too excessively hostile for games. So they have to rely on pretending to be civilized to make the conflict appear friendly. Their uncivilized nature is too hostile for their creation sports, which in itself is a type of conflict. They think that these acts of aggression or games are friendly because of their supernatural instincts, and they want to force unwanted contact with the civilized by hiding behind or concealing their attacks as games.

The current state of the world, the traumatic experiences of the civilized, the experiences of slaughtered animals, the experiences of animals waiting to be slaughtered for the consumption of the uncivilized, confirms that the uncivilized have a behavioural problem, that puts them and those around them in serious danger.

The purpose of the constitution is to regulate the behaviour of the uncivilized, because of the dangers to the civilized and the dangers to a civilized society associated with the misuse of their supernatural powers and senses.

According to the guidance of the constitution, creation is only possible by the use of supernatural powers and senses; this means that the process and the things created should be regulated by law, to protect the public from the possible misuse of supernatural powers and senses.

The uncivilized do not fall within the legal definition of a man, because of their supernatural powers and senses. Money is meant for those that fall within the legal definition of a man, the civilized. This means that no uncivilized person should have more money than any civilized person. I f the uncivilized have misused their supernatural powers and senses, to created conditions outside the instructions or guidance of the constitution to dominate the civilized, by making sure that the uncivilized will always have more money than the civilized, in order to dominate the civilized, it is treason. It is also treasonous for the uncivilized to misuse their supernatural powers and senses to always monitor how much money a civilized person can have, in order to make sure the civilized will never have enough to be comfortable, contrary to the guidance of the constitution.

The same principle is applied to insider trading or gambling, to use information that has been obtained through supernatural powers and senses to have an unfair advantage while pretending to be civilized will be regarded as fraud.

Given the pattern of behaviour of the uncivilized towards the civilized, unprovoked, illegal persecution of the civilized, any direct or indirect contact with the civilized outside the stipulated guidelines of the constitution, will be and should be interpreted as an attack. This applies regardless of how they try to manipulate appearances to create a false impression with the misuse of their supernatural powers and senses.

Anything short of the complete implementation of the instructions of the real constitution of this planet by the uncivilized is an attack on the civilized and creates hell on earth (lawlessness), contrary to the guidance of the constitution.

The uncivilized do not represent the interest of the civilized or speak for the civilized. A strict analysis of the supernatural nature of the uncivilized will confirm that they represent lawlessness, while the civilized represent or are the law. There are very serious differences which affects decisions or judgements, which suggests that the civilized and the uncivilized are completely different species, one cannot assume the role of the other.

3. WHEN DOES A CREATION BECOME A LIFE FORM WITH RIGHTS?

According to the guidance of the constitution, life can only be created supernatural. The supernatural creation of life can be done in a lot of different ways.

Once life is created supernaturally, whether the civilized or the uncivilized, they should be given a chance to live their lives, because of the constitution's guidance on the right to life. This right should not be compromised because of improper education, or compromised by being created in circumstances that are unfair, an impossible situation, which does not give them the chance to exercise their constitutional right to life. Once life has been created, the constitution requires that they should have the right to life, regardless of the intention of the creator. Once created they automatically become independent life forms that fall within the jurisdiction of the constitution's protection.

There is a pattern of behaviour of the supernatural, those with supernatural powers and senses, inflicting serious physical and mental injuries on those different from them, in most cases the infliction of fatal injuries. This is why the law is needed to better protect the vulnerable from the behavioural problems of the supernatural. Children are in constant danger from the behavioural problems of their parents. The development or education of the young is compromised, and as a consequence children are indirectly denied the opportunity to exercise their right to life.

According to the guidance of the sacred constitution, the protection of the civilized is sacred and infallible. This is an important point that the uncivilized need to be aware of, because they live an abominable life style, the uncivilized set out to conspire collectively to compromise the development or education of the civilized, in order to undermine the credibility and the constitutional rights of the civilized. The uncivilized rely on the civilized having a feeling of hopelessness and feeling isolated, which will make the civilized desperate and give in or surrender to the barbarism of the uncivilized. This policy appears to work on the uncivilized. The problem the uncivilized have with trying to do this to the civilized is that the civilized cannot naturally afford to surrender to their barbarism. This is a separate issue from the sacred protection of the civilized by the sacred constitution.

It also means that the uncivilized deliberately create life, with the intention of doing serious harm mentally or physically to the created life form.

The civilized are naturally allergic to the barbarism of the uncivilized, associated with the misuse of their supernatural powers and senses. This natural allergic reaction of the civilized to the barbarism of the uncivilized when the uncivilized misuse their supernatural powers and senses helps establish and maintain law and order. To put this simply, the civilized are naturally allergic to the constitution's real definition of criminal behaviour or activity, the misuse of supernatural powers and senses by the uncivilized. So the no nonsense approach to law enforcement by the civilized is business or natural professionalism, it is not personal.

The uncivilized have demonstrated a very hostile attitude towards the civilized, animals, and children and given their obvious disregard for all living things, their decisions regarding the creation of life has to be seriously regulated. In order to cater to their barbarism, the uncivilized have decided in line with the delusional way they live their lives, to only give a degree of importance to life created supernaturally by sexual intercourse between a man and woman, and have decided to give no importance to life created supernaturally in other ways. This decision jeopardizes the right to life of life forms(human beings) created outside the supernatural method they want to recognize, this means that other human beings created supernaturally and recognized as human beings by the real constitution but outside the method the uncivilized want to accept, are treated less favourably and exposed to abuse.

Although as someone of a civilized nature, I do not see my civilized nature as a sacrifice, the constitution in confirming the civilized as military leaders educates the uncivilized about the discipline required in establishing and maintaining world peace and security.

According to the guidance of the constitution, whether holographic images or images on television that have been supernaturally transformed to become independent living beings regardless of being representations of the images of other people, they will become independent life forms with rights under the constitution and are then entitled to exercise their right to life. This right applies regardless of the intention of the creator, if the life created is not a threat to world peace and security. The uncivilized can deliberately set out to create life as a weapon to undermine world peace and security. So, creation and the created need to be governed by law in order to maintain world peace and security.

4. AUTHOR'S NOTES

This is my fifth non-fiction book about the law. It is about what I believe to be the correct identification, interpretation and application of the constitution of this planet. The book is about a no nonsense approach to law enforcement. The uncivilized, those with supernatural powers and senses, are easily corruptible and susceptible to peer pressure which makes the need for the proper identification, interpretation and application of the law urgent, in order to establish and maintain world peace and security. My first book, The constitution and policing, is a compilation of emails I sent to the United Nations and the international criminal court regarding my concerns about the deliberate misinterpretation of the constitution of this planet by the uncivilized, resulting in the deliberate unlawful persecution of the civilized. When you have institutions or organizations like these that claim to represent the interest of the citizens of this planet, but are party to the conspiracy of the uncivilized to undermine the constitutional authority of the civilized in order to establish and maintain lawlessness, it is an abomination and has stopped the establishment of international peace and security.

5. AUTHOR'S BIOGRAPHY

My name is Lord Loveday Ememe. I was born in the United Kingdom. I am of African origin and of a civilized nature (no supernatural powers and senses). I am a graduate of an Anglican seminary school. I graduated from the University of East London with a law degree.

Bibliography

The first book of Moses: Genesis.